BMX

TRIX & TECHNIQUES

FOR THE TRACK

TONY DONALDSON

MBI

To all the friends I've made and kept in my years of involvement with the great sport of BMX,
my life is richer for your friendship.

WARNING: BMX is a dangerous sport. The riders depicted in this book are all professionals and are using proper protective gear under controlled conditions. Attempting to duplicate their actions may be hazardous. Readers are cautioned that individual abilities, bikes, racetracks, terrain, and riding conditions differ, and due to these unlimited factors beyond the control of the authors and riders quoted in this book, liability is expressly disclaimed. Do not attempt any maneuvers, stunts, or techniques that are beyond your capabilities.

First published in 2004 by MBI, an imprint of MBI Publishing Company, Galtier Plaza, Suite 200, 380 Jackson Street, St. Paul, MN 55101-3885 USA

MBI titles are also available at discounts in bulk quantity for industrial or sales-promotional use. For details write to Special Sales Manager at Motorbooks International Wholesalers & Distributors, Galtier Plaza, Suite 200, 380 Jackson Street, St. Paul, MN 55101-3885 USA.

ISBN 0-7603-1964-2

Editors: Dennis Pernu and Lindsay Hitch
Designed by: Mandy Iverson

Printed in China

On the frontispiece:
Mike Day is a master of speed jumping. He absorbs the impact with his body and keeps every ounce of momentum over the jump.

On the title page:
Things get crazy in the first turn at the X Games downhill race at Woodward West.

On the back cover:
Mike Day shows how to clear a set of doubles and stay way out front.

This young racer is sporting full protection, including a full-face helmet, jersey, racing pants, gloves, and chest protector.

About the Author: Veteran rider and photographer Tony Donaldson's photography has appeared in the likes of *ESPN the Magazine* and *Sports Illustrated for Kids*, and in print advertisements for several top shoe, clothing, and bicycle companies. An avid mountain biker, BMXer, and skateboarder, Donaldson also works in the realm of digital video and is the co-author of MBI's *The World of BMX*. He lives in the Los Angeles area.

Author Tony Donaldson, age 16, at a local track in Illinois. *Madelyn Donaldson*

CONTENTS

FOREWORD

BMX is a great sport—there are so many different ways you can spend your time riding. You can race, go to the trails and jump with your buddies, or do freestyle tricks in just about any parking lot around. One thing is for sure—it is a great way to enjoy yourself and express your individuality, regardless of what form of riding you do.

When it comes to BMX history, I cannot think of anyone with a more in-depth background than Tony Donaldson. Tony has been an editor for leading BMX publications and has his own company specializing in web design and advertising in the BMX market and beyond. His travels have brought him face to face with everyone in the BMX industry over the last 20 years and has given him the knowledge to bring you a great look into the world of BMX.

Enjoy reading this book!

Greg Hill

PREFACE

I was approached by Dennis Pernu of MBI Publishing Company to write this book after working with him and J. P. Partland on another BMX book, *The World of BMX*. Actually, Dennis asked me to write two books on BMX, one on racing and one on how to get started in freestyle BMX, simultaneously. It has been a good test of my 20-plus years in the sport as a racer, freestyler, photographer, and writer.

I really want this book to have the best information on the easiest way to get started racing BMX—the way to get out there and have fun at any level, and the tools to take it up as many notches as you'd like. Whether you just want to go to a track and check out the action or you aspire to be a top, factory-sponsored expert or pro, this book is for you.

This project was a large undertaking, and I could only think of one person to ask for advice and to check my facts: pro racer and trainer to the stars of BMX, Mr. Greg Hill. Greg and I partnered up for this book and an upcoming training video.

Thanks for taking the time to read this book, and I wish for you to reap the same lifetime of rewards and fulfillment that I have from the great sport of BMX.

ACKNOWLEDGMENTS

BMX is my favorite sport. I grew up racing and having my own freestyle team, then worked for *BMX Plus!* magazine in the late 1980s. Thanks to mentor and former *BMX Plus!* Editor, John Ker, for taking a chance on a kid from Illinois, and to my first mentor, Seth Perlman, who took me under his wing and taught me how to shoot.

I've spent my career covering BMX in one form or another for the past 16 years, and have a total of 23 years in BMX with my years racing and freestyling. BMX racing is the best family sport in the world—you won't find a nicer, more giving group of people. Everyone is in it to help everyone else have fun. From the parents who volunteer at the tracks to the racers themselves, it's one big extended family. We help each other get to the races, fix broken bikes, and take up collections for those who need help. That's probably why most people can never leave the sport and why so many kids are now second-generation racers. To my extended family, my gratitude for all you've given me and allowed me to give back.

I couldn't have done this book without the help of the best BMX trainer and arguably the greatest BMX racer of all time, Greg Hill. Not only did he dominate racing as a professional racer in the 1980s, he's since trained some of the top names in the world of BMX who have also gone on to win national titles. He races the Veteran Pro class very competitively to this day. He was my hero as a kid, and I'm very happy to call him my friend.

I must also thank my wife, Jennifer, for giving me the time to write this book. It's my first (OK, I wrote two books on BMX simultaneously) book, so there's been a bit of a learning curve over writing magazine articles, my second job behind providing photography to a lot of different outlets. Thanks also to my parents for encouraging me and driving me to races every weekend to, as my mom jokes, "watch the mud dry." Mom also gave me encouragement to be creative, helped nurture my curiosity, and taught me how to do research.

Many thanks to MBI Publishing Company for the resources, assignment, and encouragement to write the books!

INTRODUCTION

BMX racing started in 1969 and traces its roots to Scot Briethaupt and the opening sequence in a motocross movie called *On Any Sunday*.

In the 1970s it went through several changes, from Schwinn Stingrays with their easily-bent bladed forks to early, 70-pound suspension bikes to the basic form they still have today: mostly chromoly tubes, knobby tires, and increasing technology to make them stronger and lighter.

The 1980s saw the first big boom of BMX, with televised coverage of major races on the fledgling sports network ESPN and even its own movie, *Rad*. That movie has gone on to cult status, and shortly after it came out another rarity called *BMX The Movie* was released in Australia (known as *BMX Bandits* here in the States if you can find it on VHS). That movie was far less popular, but was the first movie in the career of one Nicole Kidman.

The magazines and coverage of the 1980s gave rise to many of the sport's most celebrated stars: guys like Stu Thomsen, Greg Hill, Brent and Brian Patterson, Harry Leary, and many others.

The sport continued to progress through the lean years of the 1990s and has since come back to popularity thanks to more coverage on videos, television, and especially the X Games.

It's a sport of individual accomplishment; you're neither carried nor held back by a team, you can be as good as you commit yourself to being. One thing is for sure, almost everyone who gets involved heavily in BMX becomes a "BMXer;" it's a lifestyle more than a sport. You'll want to be on your bike 24/7, racing, goofing off with your buds, or whatever. People joke about eating, thinking, and sleeping a particular sport, but BMX is truly that addictive. There wasn't a high school class that I didn't have at least one BMX magazine with me.

Riding with my friends every day was a given. Whether playing chicken, building jumps, or riding out to the track for practice, we rode almost every single day, even in snow and ice, having distance sliding contests on frozen ponds.

Your friends in BMX will be your friends for life.

This is an open-face helmet with a mouth guard. This helmet offers the best skid protection for your chin and mouth if you go over the bars.

CHAPTER 1
HOW TO GET STARTED

BMX is a great sport. In many ways, it seems to be the only lifelong sport of all the action sports. Many people skateboard as kids, but give it up by adulthood. Most of the people I know who raced BMX as kids continue racing today, even as they take their own kids racing. It's a really fantastic sport for entire families.

It's a great way to make new friends, too. I got my first BMX bike for Christmas one year, and when I rode it to school a few days later my entire circle of friends shifted and I had a whole new group of people to hang out with. It was awesome—my life completely changed. We'd ride every day after school and spend all day thinking about riding. I usually had at least one copy of *BMX Action* (a magazine without equal, which unfortunately no longer exists) with me at every class.

After school we'd ride trails and hit jumps, have races over urban terrain (One way to make sure your bunnyhopping skills are at their best!), or go to somebody's ramp. We loved building ramps. Freestyle was just getting popular, and we started making backyard quarterpipes and learning how to get air.

We all decided to try racing at an actual BMX track, and since a couple of us knew where it was, we went out one weekend to check it out. Just watching it I knew I was hooked. So did everyone else in the group. It's such a rush, the gate slamming down and eight riders blasting out, flying around the track. The skill some of the guys have is incredible, being able to get speed out of every part of the track.

I brought out my parents right after that to sign me up and their lives changed, too. Suddenly, we were at a nearby track almost every weekend. My friends and I rode every day and sometimes we'd even ride to the track for practice. My mom still jokes that our hobby was going out to a different track every weekend to watch the mud dry (it rains a lot in the Midwest, where I grew up).

One reason that BMX is such a great family sport is because your family becomes part of the larger BMX family. Everybody helps everybody else, from driving to the track to loaning parts to working in the infield. I've seen tracks take up a collection to help replace a stolen bike or to help pay doctor bills for an injury or illness. BMX families on the local and national level all seem to be the same kind of helpful, friendly people interested only in making every weekend a fun one.

Finding your local track can be as easy as asking at your local bike shop. You can find a complete list of tracks by checking with the local sanctioning bodies. In the United States, you can check out the National Bicycle League (NBL) online at www.nbl.org or by calling (617) 777-1625. The American Bicycle Association (ABA) is online at www.ababmx.com (you'll have to use Internet Explorer, no other browser will work) and can also be reached by calling (602) 961-1903. Both websites include listings of tracks, national events, rules, and contact information if you need more information.

The ABA and NBL run their races a little differently. The ABA uses the transfer system, so if you place high enough in the moto you don't have to race again until the mains. The NBL uses the moto system, so your average of three races earns you either your place (if there are eight riders or less in a class) or your berth in a semi or main. Both systems are valid and good, but on big race days under the transfer system you can get bored waiting for a main if you qualify in the first round of motos.

The NBL has a special just to get you started—they'll give you the information on your local track and send you a package that includes a coupon for a free race, a copy of their publication (*BMX Today*), and some cool stickers, all at no charge. If you like your first race, you can sign up and pay the membership fee and you're ready to start your career as a racer.

The ABA has a beginner kit for $25 that includes a 30-day membership to race as much as you want in any single-point races. Your points don't count with this beginner membership, but if you then sign up for a full membership, the $25 you paid as a beginner is applied to the full membership fee.

Go to their websites or call them and find out where the nearest track is, and contact the track for race and practice schedules. You can go on race days and see all the excitement, and go on practice days to try it out yourself. Some tracks have beginner clinics, in which a group of beginners (and sometimes even more advanced racers) can learn better techniques. Some clinics are run by top experts at the track, and some are run by experts who travel from track to track. Former number-one pro Greg Hill, arguably one of the best racers of all time, travels all over the country teaching clinics that cover beginner through pro-level training. You can find more information about his schedule at www.greghillspeedseminars.com. He also teaches private clinics and coaches racers via an online program.

There are tons of ways to learn, but the most important thing is to get out to a track, try racing for yourself, and have fun!

CHOOSING A BIKE

If you haven't already gotten a bike, here are a few words of advice.

If your friends all have bikes, and love a specific brand, that may be your choice. Brand favorites come and go, but the best part is that most manufacturers know how to make bikes that ride extremely well. If you want, pick up some of the magazines and read up on what's out there. *BMX Plus!*, *Ride*, and *Transworld BMX* are great magazines and good places to start. Most of them produce an annual buyer's guide filled to the brim with the best information on the latest bikes and gear. Reading up on that stuff is half the fun.

When you're ready to buy your first bike, find a shop near you that specializes in BMX. They'll have the latest bikes and the know-how to help pick a setup for you. Usually, if you're 14 or older, bikes right off the rack can work well for you. The important thing about a bike shop, though, is the service. You'll always have a place to bring the bike for repairs, maintenance, new parts, and advice. The guys there may not seem as young and hip as you, but they've been around bikes a long time and that experience can go a long way toward helping you choose bikes and parts that will last and work well for a long time.

This rider has gloves and saves his chin by keeping his helmet off the ground. The long pants are good, but padded racing pants would provide even more protection in a fall.

Many younger riders customize their bikes to lighten them up, from smaller frames and narrower wheels to aluminum cranks and bars. Once, for an article in *BMX Plus!,* we made a bike that was all titanium, right down to the chain and spokes. It was awesome—super strong, super light (Nine pounds!), and virtually bulletproof. But it also cost *$10,000.* You'll never have to go that crazy to make a bike light and competitive.

A good, top pro race bike weighs around 24 or 25 pounds and is really sturdy. A bike made for jumping and trail riding tends to be much heavier, with features like three-piece chrome-moly cranks and triple-walled rims. Race bikes need to

be lighter. And the rotating weight (wheels, cranks, etc.) is three times more critical than the non-rotating weight (like the frame). For a good racer, aluminum frames and carbon fiber forks can make life easier—just don't use them for your backyard jumps.

The extent to which you lighten or otherwise trick out your bike depends on your needs. If you're a really competitive, national-level racer, you probably have sponsors providing the latest and greatest gear. If you race weekends locally, like most of us, you likely don't need anything fancy. I used to race against a guy who had a good frameset, but everything else on his bike was pretty cheap. We'd goof on him, but he'd smoke us on the track and just riding around in general. He proved that it wasn't about the bike, but all about the guy riding it. Mat Hoffman once had his bike stolen at the airport while on his way to the X Games. He went to a bike shop nearby that carried his bikes, grabbed one off the rack (He even left the CPSC reflectors on!) and rode as well as he always rides. It was a testament to how well his bikes are straight off the rack, for sure, but it also proved that you don't need to wait 'til you have the perfect bike to race.

SAFETY GEAR

After you get a bike, you'll also need some safety gear to be able to race. First, you'll need (and want) a good set of pads for your bike. Though the ABA specifies that you must have pads on the top tube, handlebar crossbar, and stem, the NBL takes it a step further and specifies that those pads must also be at least 1/4-inch thick. Many race bikes come with, or have as an option, a set of matching pads. If not, get a set that's made by a good company. You can also be creative and pick a set that fits your particular style. Just remember to get good ones. They'll last longer and protect you when you need it most.

The strongest protection you can get for your elbows and forearms is a separate, made-for-BMX pad. It can be hot and somewhat restrictive, but it can also be a big confidence booster.

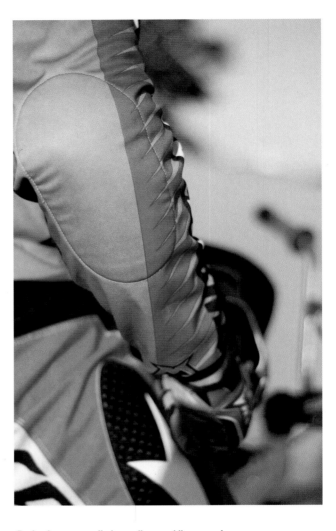

Racing jerseys usually have elbow padding sewn in.

At the minimum, clothing must include a long-sleeve shirt and long pants ("waist to ankles," per NBL wording). Any long-sleeve shirt and jeans will work. I've even seen guys race in sweat pants. The track operator may let you do this, but I wouldn't recommend it. If you fall you really have no protection. If you have the bucks, properly designed racing jerseys and racing pants are the hot ticket. They offer total flexibility, sewn-in padding, and plenty of breathability. They're also really lightweight. You can pick ones like the risers on your favorite team wear, or you can even get your own custom made.

Shoes? Flat, soft-soled tennis shoes work fine, or you can get shoes specifically for BMX. If you're riding clipless pedals (which you actually clip into), you'll need shoes with cleats that work with the type of pedals you have. Some pedals have adjustable mounts for various styles of cleats. For beginners, it's better to start off with regular platform or caged pedals until you get to the level of racing where clips can become an advantage.

Your helmet is the one thing where you want to spend the money and make sure you get a great one. Bell Sports had a memorable marketing campaign years ago that said, "If you have a $10 head, buy a $10 helmet." It's marketing, but it's also very true. You can beat up any other part of your body, but if you rattle your head enough you'll have nothing inside it but a bunch of useless mush. Check out the latest styles, talk to the people at the bike shop, and find one that fits comfortably, is made for what you're doing (you don't need a motorcycle helmet), and gives you full field of view. Full-face helmets, those with the mouth guard molded into them, are good for high-impact situations (ramps, huge jumps, etc.), but aren't always the best choice for racing. Most racers these days seem to choose them, but in normal racing I've seen more kids cut

This full-face helmet offers stronger protection for your mouth and jaw if you slam face first. But if you land more on your chest first, this style can pop up and leave the chin exposed to scraping the dirt.

Here's a kid with full protection, including a full-face helmet, jersey, racing pants, gloves, and chest protector.

Lining up for motos gives you time to get your head straight, visualize the perfect race, and stretch a bit to get ready.

their chins open in falls while wearing full-face models. If you do fall forward onto your face, these helmets can flip up enough to expose the chin. An open-face helmet with a mouth guard, on the other hand, offers a wider field of view and better protection in the most common types of crashes.

Other protection to consider, though not required, includes gloves, goggles, and chest protectors.

Gloves are always a good choice, since they protect your hands in a fall and help keep your sweaty palms from slipping off your grips. You can spend any amount, but a lot of manufacturers make relatively inexpensive gloves, like Pryme's "Trailhands," which sell for around $16. Try several types and see which ones feel best.

Goggles or sunglasses protect your eyes from the bright sun, all the dust and dirt, and whatever else might be flying about. Goggles are also nice

Nobody says you have to get the full factory gear to race. This racer has a helmet and jersey, but opts for jeans over racing pants.

These guys have the full factory look with jerseys and racing pants. Looking at the style of riding and the sponsored clothing, you can tell these racers are experts.

because you can get different lenses for sunny days, night racing, and indoor racing. Sunglasses and glasses work fine, as well.

Chest protectors are good crash protection. Not only do they protect your chest and back from the harsh ground and all the metal bike parts that might jab you in a crash, they can also help protect your collarbones in cases where you fall more on your shoulders. Nothing can guarantee you won't break a bone, but things like chest protectors help spread the impact over a

If you practice and train, these are what you'll get...

larger area, lessening the shock to the body and decreasing the likelihood of injury.

As for other requirements, both the NBL and ABA have rulebooks they can send to you. They're also available as pdf files on both sites, easily readable with Adobe Acrobat Reader (a free download from www.adobe.com if your computer doesn't already have it).

SPONSORSHIP

Sponsorship is a subject that becomes an obsession among many riders. Because the top experts and pros all have sponsors, *everyone* wants to be sponsored. How great would that be if you had someone who would fly you to races, give you free bikes and gear, and in some cases *pay* you to race? It's every kid's dream. But it can happen only if you have the raw determination to be that competitive. You have to be really committed and race a lot to get there.

In the meantime, have fun. If you start getting good and winning races but you're not at the national level yet, consider asking local businesses to sponsor you and maybe another couple of racers as a team. It gets outside companies involved which is always a good thing since they often help support the local track and vice-versa.

Look at this happy kid—the trophy is as big as he is!

Gate starts are the single most important part of the race.

CHAPTER 2
GATE STARTS

The gate start can be the most important part of the race. A perfect start gives you momentum and gets you out in front of the pack. Getting the lead out of the gate is called the "hole shot," and gives you control of everyone to the first turn.

The mechanics of a good gate start are relatively simple, and with practice, can be easy to achieve regularly.

But before getting to the gate, you first have to get in line behind the gate. If you're just starting out, this is a place to socialize, and that's fine. But in the upper levels of racing—expert and pro—you'll get into a more solitary place while there. Most pros and top experts concentrate on clearing their minds and running the race in their heads, over and over again, perfectly, so that when they get to the gate they know exactly what to do and how to do it.

Not a bad plan for when you're starting out, either. This pre-visualization, drawing on your memory of the track from riding in practice, is the best way to "get in your game" and be able

to blast out of the gate and win races. Some light stretching to keep warm and limber also helps.

On your way up to the gate, watch several starts. Learn the cadence, the "Riders ready, watch the lights!" Then watch the lights and see how they're timed. Have your hands on the bars, and pull on them to learn to time your snap.

Once you're at the gate, go for a two-pedal start. Most gates are metal mesh, so knobby tires (e.g., Tioga Comp III, the standard for many years) will grab the mesh and make balancing easier. You can practice this beforehand by putting your front wheel against a wall and putting pressure on your forward pedal to press your front tire against the wall. If you can balance on a slick wall for a few minutes at a time, balancing at the actual gate will be easier and you can concentrate on your start.

Center your bike on the gate. Having it offset on the gate will put you in the wrong place or put you into the rider in the next lane when you come out of the gate. Relax. Take a few deep

Before staging, everyone who has a moto coming up is gathers nearby to get their assigned gate positions and prepares to go into staging.

While in staging, spend as much time as you can mentally preparing for the race.

Don't bend your wrist like this. It's too relaxed and won't give you maximum pull when the gate drops.

This is proper hand and wrist position—straight in line with your arm. You can get maximum power in your pull on the bars as you crank off the gate.

breaths. Level your pedals; usually the rear pedal will be even with the front or one or two free-wheel clicks below the chain stays. Uneven pedals will make it too hard to get the all-important first pedal. Lean back. Beginners tend to lean forward too much. Leaning just behind center allows you to throw your hips forward and crush into your first pedal, giving you a burst of momentum out of the gate.

Your hands on the grips should be firm, but relaxed. Wrists should be fairly straight so you can pull hard on the bars.

When the gate drops, throw your hips forward (your hips should nearly hit the bars as you throw your weight forward), pull hard on the bars, and throw your first pedal toward China. Get that momentum going and carry it through the first several pedals.

The first three to four pedals are crucial to a good start and can mean the difference between an early lead and getting stuck in the pack. Do not hit the gate with the front tire. If you can, follow it down exactly. Hitting it an inch or two behind is better than hitting it on the way down, which can seriously impede your momentum. In extreme cases hitting the gate with your weight going forward can cause you to endo, or flip over the bars. There's almost no way you can win your moto if you are on the ground at the gate when the other seven riders are through the first turn.

Here's a quick advanced tip. Don't look at the gate lights. Look down at the gate and use your peripheral vision to keep an eye on the lights. Peripheral vision offers much better reaction time. If the lights are a series of red, yellow, yellow, green, and you know you have to start your snap right as the second yellow lights, keeping an eye indirectly on it helps you with exact timing on the lights and lets you blast out of the gate and get the hole shot.

Bubba Harris, one of the fastest guys on two wheels, shows how to win a race from the start with excellent gate starting form. He's running through the race while sitting and waiting on the cadence to start.

002

This is the second light right before the green. Bubba's already starting to pull hard with his right arm and throw his weight forward.

003

Bubba's weight is almost fully forward; he's pulled his front wheel up to clear the gate and he's cranking his right pedal down like his life depends on it.

Almost through the first pedal, Bubba's head is down, he's pulling hard and setting up for the next pedal.

Bubba is going into his second critical pedal, just thinking about getting ahead of everyone. His head starts to come up as his back wheel goes across the gate.

He shifts his weight more to the center of the bike as his front wheel comes down.

Bubba's weight is fully on the left pedal, forcing it down as hard as he did on the first pedal.

008

As Bubba gets into his third pedal he's looking straight ahead. He's already 6 to 8 inches ahead of the rider next to him, about 1/2 second into the race.

Rich Carolan demonstrates a good gate start. Even with 24-inch cruisers the technique is the same.

He's up and waiting as the cadence starts.

010

Rich waits with his weight back, ready to snap.

Though not everyone does this, Rich has his hands relaxed on the gate just before it drops. He's listening to the cadence as it starts.

As the red light goes and the gate releases, Rich throws his weight forward and pulls hard on the bars. This is anticipation and timing at its best.

The gate is down a split second later and he's on the bottom of his first pedal.

Treat the second pedal like the first and push hard.

As Rich enters his third pedal, he's looking ahead on the track and concentrating on accelerating.

Increasing his speed, Rich concentrates on his line.

He's starting to set up for the first jump.

He's still accelerating, jump or no jump, aiming for the first turn.

Younger riders are allowed to have help from a parent if they're unable to do a two-pedal start on their own.

These young experts have already mastered proper start form.

Little guys may not blast out of the gate as fast as the bigger ones, but a good gate start is a good gate start no matter what the age.

LEFT: No matter your size or age, a good gate is important. Here veteran Tom Ehrnsdorf shows excellent form.

The metal mesh provides plenty of grip. This part of the race is like putting is to golf—about 40 percent of the race is won or lost right here.

Once you have the hole shot, it's up to you to protect your lead.

Sitting with your legs spread wide, stretch toward one foot. Keep your knee locked and flat, and don't bounce. Hold for 20 to 30 seconds and then stretch toward the other foot.

STRETCHING

Stretching is as important as any other part of training. If you do nothing else between race days and on race days, you should stretch. It not only warms up your muscles and gets the blood flowing everywhere it needs to, it also helps you avoid injury, gain range of motion, and ensures your muscles are as strong as they can be.

The first thing you get with stretching is a flush of blood to the muscles. This helps eliminate lactic acid. If you feel soreness in your muscles after a workout, it's because of a buildup of lactic acid. Stretching also pushes all the nutrients and oxygen you need into the muscles.

The increased range of motion will help you on every part of the track, and if you crash, the flexibility you gain can mean a much lower chance for injuries, like torn muscles. Muscle tears can take a long, painful time to heal.

Stretch straight forward from the same position. You can grab grass or the carpet to assist your stretch.

You can't have maximum strength in a given muscle if it isn't flexible and able to work in its full range of motion.

If you take two people who are on the same training program and one stretches while the other doesn't, the one who stretches will be easily 10 to 15 percent stronger because that person's muscles are getting everything they need. You want to warm up and stretch before a race or practice so you can get everything out of your body on the track.

There are a lot of different stretches you can do. We'll cover just a few here.

Begin seated. Bring your feet as far apart as you can and keep your legs flat on the floor. Stretch toward each foot and hold for 20 to 30 seconds at a time. Do not bounce when you stretch. Bouncing is also known as ballistic stretching and it can easily tear your muscles, sometimes without you even knowing it. Go with a slow, deliberate stretch.

Next, begin in the standing position. Keep your legs locked and a little more than shoulder-width apart. Stretch toward each foot slowly, again holding for 20 to 30 seconds. Mix it up a little by reaching your hands behind you through your legs as far as you can comfortably hold it. Stretch your hands forward and feel the stretch in your hamstrings (large muscles on the upper back of your legs) and your back.

Next, stretch your triceps (muscles on the back of your arm) and shoulders by grabbing your elbow and pulling it behind your head. For a side stretch, stand about shoulder-width apart. Place one hand on your hip and stretch the other arm over toward the side with your hand on your hip.

Last but not least, stretch your quadriceps (the muscles on the front of your upper leg). These are the muscles you need to be the strongest when you're pedaling like crazy around the track. Stand comfortably, and you can certainly lean on a wall for this one, grabbing one foot with the opposite hand and pulling the foot up behind you. Hold 20 to 30 seconds each side.

Any and all of these should be done several times per body part. Almost any movement that can stretch some part of your body is good. There are tons of books and lots of information online about stretching if you're curious.

Try to stretch before and after every workout. Twenty minutes a day can make you very flexible and keep you at the maximum level of fitness. Twenty minutes of stretching may sound like a lot, but a few minutes before and a few minutes after your workout is easy. And if you watch television, try sitting on the floor and stretching while you watch, even if just during commercials. Stretching when you first get up in the morning will get you moving and start your whole day better.

01

Standing with your feet a little more than shoulder-width apart, stretch toward your right foot and hold for 20 to 30 seconds. Repeat toward your left foot as well.

02

From that position, stretch your hands out forward as far as you can onto the floor and hold.

03

Stretch back behind you.

04

This is a good stretch for your triceps (the muscles on the back of your upper arms). Make sure to stretch both arms well.

05

Keep your feet about shoulder-width apart with one hand on your hip, then stretch the other arm over as far as you can. This stretch loosens up your midsection and side.

06

Stretching the quadriceps is easy and can help prevent a really painful tear if you fall with your leg under you. Stand on your right leg; grab your left foot with your right hand and pull up to feel a gentle stretch. Hold 20 to 30 seconds, then switch.

SPRINT TRAINING

To train yourself for great gates, you can practice a variety of things. Balancing against a wall helps with balance and relaxation on the gate. You can never practice enough, and going to the track on practice nights will help also. On race days, get as many gates as you can, sprinting out three to four pedals then coasting the rest of the track to get used to it (if it's an unfamiliar track) so you don't get overtired.

Some people build or buy small one- to two-person gates. These can be expensive, but are a convenient way to practice gates away from the track.

Sprint training will help you have better starts. Set up two markers—a start and a finish (they can be two sticks, cracks in the pavement, plastic soda bottles, or anything else you can safely use)—about 30 feet apart. You don't need a whole track's worth, just four to five pedals' worth. Ride up to the first mark, stall there, and balance on the pedals, then snap like you're coming out of the gate. Do these one after another, with a few seconds to rest between. The more practice, the merrier—but don't kill yourself the first few times. Over-training breaks down your body more than it builds it up. If you don't have time to rest and heal between practice sessions your body can actually get weaker instead of stronger.

Practice with a variety of lengths. Start out at 40 yards, then go to about 70 yards, and work your way up to 120 yards. Top riders can do six or seven of the 120-yard sprints or ten to twelve of the 70-yard sprints before being really tired, even with a two-minute rest between sprints. Make sure you rest between sprints. You're not trying for endurance; you want to train your body specifically for quick, short bursts. This kind of training is the foundation of a top racer's training routine. If you can do this three days a week, you can become one of the best.

07

Sprints are an easy and important part of training. They get your legs and body ready to blast off from the gate. Do 10 to 12 short 40- to 70-yard all-out sprints with a two-minute rest between.

Greg lines up and imagines the cadence and lights at the gate.

09

Starting is just like a gate start without the gate or the hill.

10

This will train your body to really crank off gates; it's harder on flat ground.

11

Just like a gate start, hit your second pedal as hard as the first.

12

Greg can crank hard enough to keep his front wheel off the ground for nearly the entire sprint.

13

This is a short sprint, but it's enough to be effective if you give it everything you've got.

14

When you hit the end, take a couple of slower pedals and coast back around to cool down.

In the freestyle world, jumps are for getting air. In the racing world, the idea is to use your body to suck up the jump and keep the power on the ground.

CHAPTER 3
SPEED JUMPS

SINGLE JUMPS

Basic speed jumping entails riding up to the jump, going full speed, and getting as much power going into the jump as you can. At the last possible second, stop pedaling and relax, and then set up for the next step. Keep your pedals level; pump them slightly if you have to. Pull up your front wheel—basically unweight it and let the jump help you. Keep your legs relaxed and let the bike come up into your body.

Stay low; you don't want to get a lot of air. You need to keep the bike on the ground as much as you can to get power, whether it's pedal power or using your body to gain speed. Think of your upper body trying to travel in the straightest line possible. The main mass of your body is the heaviest, so you want to keep that inertia going in a straight line to be the most efficient.

Getting a lot of air looks cool when you're riding trails, but in a race that's going to get you passed really easily.

As you crest the jump, tuck your rear as far back as you can and let the back wheel come up toward it. Think of trying to kiss the seat really quickly. You can absorb the jump and be ready for the boost of speed you'll get on the backside of the jump. Keep your body as loose as you can and let the jump do most of the work for you.

If the jump is really big, you can pedal down the backside. If it's smaller, just use your body and force the back wheel to stay on the backside and go down hard. By forcing it down the back of the jump it actually builds speed, something that can really be to your advantage. Have your finger on your rear brake lever so that if you feel like you're going to loop out (fall backwards) you can tap your brake to drop the front end and keep control.

This is a basic small roller jump. Sometimes these are placed one after another to form a rhythm section.

Tabletop jumps have a front side, a back side, and a flat crest that can be fairly long.

001

Rolling jumps teach beginning racers good speed-jumping technique.

Double jumps are simply known as doubles. Depending on your comfort level and what's happening in the race, you can roll, manual, or jump these.

Stay loose and let your bike follow the ground as your body tries to stay at about the same level, which keeps your momentum going in a straight line.

003

Let the bike roll downhill and try to push it down with your body to help gain momentum.

004

005

At the bottom of the jumps, preload a little to help as you pull your way up the front side of the next jump. The more you pump these, the faster you can get over them and build speed.

006

As the bike rolls up the jump, let it come into your body, absorbing the jump.

007

As you pass over the jump, tuck back and get ready to push down on the back side again.

Preload at the bottom of the jump.

If it's a gradual incline and not a jump, set up and get back to pedaling as soon as possible.

DOUBLE JUMPS

If you're going over a double jump, it's okay to get a little air over the gap between the two jumps. Don't be intimidated by actually jumping during a race. You want to take off on the top of the first jump and get just enough air to make it across and land smoothly on the backside of the second. You want to come down at the top of the second one so you can push down and gain speed on the back. Have your front wheel slightly below level, but land so that your rear wheel hits just before your first.

Jumping a double is one of the few times you'll want to leave the ground in a race. Perfectly clearing a set of doubles is key to getting as much speed as you can while you race.

011

As you take off, pull up enough to fully clear the set.

012

The apex of the jump is where you know if you'll make it or not.

Mid-air corrections are possible; a little movement on the bike sets up for landing.

It's ideal to set up to land smoothly on the top of the back side of the jump.

Land your bike at about the same angle as the back of the second double, or land the front wheel just before.

Greg lands front-wheel-first, something that's not as good as landing both wheels at the same time.

Absorb the landing and crouch to set up to push down hard on the back side of the jump to gain speed.

Here's an easy technique you can use in practice that can save you from a trip over the bars during the race:

Pick a smaller double with a reasonable distance between the two tops of the jumps. Approach at moderate speed and jump it. If you land a little short, have your front wheel fairly high up and your body relaxed, legs bent. Make sure the front wheel clears the top of the second double. Your front wheel will come down right after the back wheel hits. As long as it makes it over the jump and you're relaxed, you'll make it.

Keep trying to jump a little farther and a little farther until you can clear the small double comfortably. Then start trying the other doubles on the track, working your way up to the biggest ones. Don't jump anything you're not comfortable jumping. Crashing on the bigger jumps is dangerous, and the dirt on a BMX track is nearly as hard and unforgiving as cement.

Learning to 50/50 a jump is a great skill and an easy way to learn to fully clear doubles. It also teaches you how to handle coming up short in a race.

018

019

As you take off, have enough speed to clear the double.

020

Keep your front wheel up.

021

Keep your weight up and the front wheel high as you go through the air.

It can be nerve-racking to approach the landing a little short, but following Greg's simple lesson will make you fearless in no time.

022

023

As you land on the front side of the second double, let your back wheel come down first and keep your weight behind center.

024

When your back wheel lands, focus on letting the front wheel clear the top of the second double.

025

Stay loose and let the back wheel roll over the top of the jump as your front wheel touches down.

026

Tuck back to absorb the jump.

As you go down the back side of the jump, get in position to push the bike down hard just like you would for a good speed jump.

At the bottom, you should be pedaling or setting up for the next jump or turn.

RHYTHM SECTIONS

A rhythm section is a straightaway with one jump after another, often six or eight jumps in a row. The first thing you have to do is learn to roll over them. Keep your body loose, start slow, and work your way up. It's basically the same thing as a single jump, but there are a lot of them in a row. Typically, you won't be able to pedal through a rhythm section. There may be small double jumps that you can either roll or jump. Practicing on each track is important so you can find the best "rhythm" of rolling and jumping in the rhythm section.

Use your body to control your speed over the jumps—suck up the front of each jump, and force your bike down hard on the back of the jump so you can get some good pump going and actually increase your speed!

The fastest guys will "manual" the entire section—that is, pull up the front wheel and roll over the whole thing with the front wheel up, pushing the back wheel down the backside of every jump, building speed throughout the entire section. Some of the top pros and experts can actually manual jump over the doubles in the rhythm sections of a track. It's amazing to watch, and these guys are almost always the ones who are out in front of everyone else.

Manualing is like speed jumping on steroids. Keep your front wheel up over several jumps, and force your back wheel down the back sides of jumps to gain speed.

027

To learn to manual, you can set up off a jump. Roll up the front side like a normal roller.

Let your front wheel come up, and let your weight come back enough to find your balance point.

Use your legs to force the back wheel down to gain speed. Be ready with your back brake if you start to loop out.

At the bottom of the jump, you have to be centered on the back wheel balance point and ready for the next jump.

031

032

When you're learning, stick to manualing short distances.

Even while learning, when you roll, speed jump, or manual, always pump the jumps to get the most speed you can.

As you learn the proper technique and rhythm, you'll really get a lot out of manualing.

This rider looks pretty stylish, though he's actually a little crooked, losing a bit of momentum for his style.

Proper jumping will get you ahead of the pack and powering down the back sides of even the bigger jumps.

Though getting the hole shot can put you in front, clean speed jumping can keep you there.

Riders of all abilities can learn to speed jump well. Stay low and keep cranking.

Mike Day shows how to clear a set of doubles and stay way out front.

You can roll doubles if you're not comfortable jumping them. Keeping forward momentum is much faster than hanging up if you can't clear the jumps.

Mike Day is a master of speed jumping. Note how he absorbs the impact and keeps every ounce of momentum over the jump.

Though this guy is a little stiff, he's still able to clear a double and keep most of his speed.

Some riders like to show off during the race if they have a big enough lead. It looks cool but it can cost you the lead if you squirrel out.

Another shot of Mike Day, this time during practice, working on his manual technique over a double. Look how far back he's tucked for maximum control and power when needed.

Manualing takes practice. This rider is standing a little high, making it harder to control and keep the manual up, and cutting the amount of power that can be put into the push on the back side of the jump.

This simple plyometric exercise will strengthen your legs for explosive power on the track.

PLYOMETRICS

Plyometric jumping helps you with stamina and explosive power around the track. It's a really simple move you can do almost anywhere (except maybe where you might hit your head on the ceiling) and any time without special equipment.

Start out standing with your feet shoulder-width apart. Have your hands and arms outstretched to the sides at about a 45-degree angle downward. Bend your knees and let your upper body come down slowly. At the bottom, fully squat down so your fingers just touch the ground. Keep your head up and your upper body straight.

As your fingers touch, explode and jump up as high as you can. When you're in the air, your legs should be completely straight. When your feet hit the ground again, use your legs to absorb the impact and bring yourself back down, slow and controlled. You're working the fast-twitch muscle fibers, the ones that give you the most power when you ride.

Coming down slowly is kind to your knees. Trust me; you want to be good to them. Knees are weak spots on everyone's body. As you're coming down, roll your feet up onto your toes as your fingers near the ground. This gives you better balance and will help work more of your leg. As you blast up again, drive your toes through the ground. This helps work your calves; it's a sort of calf raise.

Do four to five sets of as many reps as you can. Pause three to four minutes between each set. Walk around between sets. You want to keep your legs moving—don't sit down. Wear a watch so your resting is consistent. Consistency is the key to improving through training. For this exercise you want to raise your heart rate then let it come back down. This also helps prepare you for the sprinting involved with BMX. Plyometric jumps are the best training you can do for explosive power in your racing.

Start from a standing position.

Squat down with your arms out for balance.

Push your feet into the ground like you're driving them to China.

05

Start to spring up.

06

Use your legs to propel yourself up with everything you've got.

07

Go for height.

08

As you come up, push off your toes to add work for your calves.

At the apex, your arms should still be outstretched and your toes pointed down.

You're off the ground at this point; this is your follow-through.

11

12

Hold your position as you start to come down.

13

Prepare to land on the balls of your feet first.

As you touch down, try to land as light as you can and start to slow your descent.

14

Come down slow and controlled.

15

Try to quickly line up for the next jump.

Get in position and hold it for a second to make sure you have your balance. Repeat.

When you're down, your hands should be out at your sides barely touching the ground or just above.

This is the starting point for plyometrics. Make sure you're up on the balls of your feet, your back is fairly straight, and your legs are ready to spring.

Rich Carolan shows good form railing around a berm.

CHAPTER 4
TURNS

Turns in BMX are usually tall, banked turns called berms. They're an important part of the track and can provide the easiest way to pass other riders.

The basic idea is to crank hard into the berm, carve through or pass, and then exit with as much speed as possible, putting yourself in the best possible position for the next jump. You want to keep your weight pretty much centered, with a little more weight on the outside pedal so the inside is ready to crank hard and get you out of the turn.

Your weight should also be evenly distributed between the wheels so that both tires get as much traction as possible. Too much weight on the back wheel can cause your front wheel to wash out. Put too much on the front wheel, and your back wheel can slide and won't have enough grip when you crank out of the corner.

Techniques have changed a little over the years, since most riders have gone from platform pedals to "clipless" (ironically, you actually do "clip in" to clipless pedals using special cleats). Clipless pedals allow you to pull up with your back foot while pushing down with your front foot on each pedal stroke. It's more efficient, but it can also be a little scarier when you consider that it's a lot harder to get your feet off of the pedals if you have to. Usually, you want to stay on the pedals. The more you can be ready to pedal, the better off you are. In most cases, other than tight, off-camber (flat) turns, you don't want

Rich Carolan powers through a turn. Years ago, his front wheel would have come up a lot higher, but now that racers are "clipped in," the front wheel comes up very little out of a turn.

Whether you're going through a turn with one other person or the whole pack, the techniques are the same.

to take your feet off the pedals at all. In the 1980s, I used to race pavement-and-wood indoor tracks in the winter. There, you had to drag your inside foot on the floor for balance—and the leg out was not only a good balancing point, it was also a good blocking device.

Turns, in general, slow you down, so you want to be able to get back on the power as soon as you can. Go into each turn knowing what you want to do. This includes planning for the other riders' actions. If you get a bad start and are going into the first turn behind everyone, keep your eyes open. The first turn is always crowded, so if it looks like there's going to be a pileup, going way outside can sometimes get you around it and keep you from getting stuck in the mess.

If you're out front or in the pack, here are some ways around the other guys.

Bubba Harris has to know almost by feel where Alexis Vergara (No. 9) and the rest of the pack are to avoid getting passed.

RAILING THE TURN

If you're in the lead, you have complete control of where you go and how you get there. Pedal hard into the turn. Head for the inside part first, about 2 to 3 feet from the inside white line. Briefly stop pedaling and shift your weight toward the outside of the turn. As soon as you get to the center or apex of the turn, pedal hard and build as much speed as you can—there's usually a jump or a rhythm section not too far after the turn, sometimes immediately after it.

If you're not in the lead, you've got to pass somebody to get ahead. Turns are the best place to do this, and with a little practice, you can learn to go by people pretty easily in these track sections.

Greg Hill shows the fastest way through the turn. Pedal in hard.

You can stop pedaling for a few seconds at the middle as you shift your weight outside

From here, you can judge your speed by feel.

At this point, you'll know whether to brake or get ready to pedal.

Get ready to pedal.

008

As you get start to leave the berm, start pedaling.

009

010

Pedal hard out to set up for the next jump.

011

Pick a line to follow.

012

If there's no one around you, the line can be anywhere.

013

If there is someone behind you, you'll have to stay in front of them.

Use the end of the berm like a mini starting hill.

Get out of there and head for what's next.

THE HIGH-LOW PASS

The rider ahead of you will usually try to stay toward the middle of the turn. The high-low pass is the way to go from the outside to the inside and swoop under the rider in front of you.

Start by cranking hard and heading outside, higher on the berm than the rider you want to pass. If they can see you coming, they'll often steer higher to block. In general, the rider in front of you will edge toward the higher part of the berm as he goes through anyway.

As you approach the rider's back tire, if you're outside it, you can almost let your front tire pass his if you'd like. When you get to the halfway point of the berm, it's time to make your move. Tap your brake to slow yourself enough to turn and dive down to the inside of the other rider and then lay on the gas. You'll find your speed increases as you go underneath at a steeper angle and pass on the inside. If you can get far enough ahead before the end of the turn, cut back over and close the door (block the rider you just passed) so they can't pass you in turn.

016

In the high-low pass, set up outside (higher than) the person you want to pass. Here, Greg Hill goes into the turn on the outside of Rich Carolan.

017 Pedal as long as you can into the turn.

018 Carry enough speed to pass.

019 As the person ahead is still climbing up the berm to hold you back, start to carve down.

020 You have to carve quickly; if they see you do it, they can try to cut inside and hold you back.

021

Pedal for all you're worth as you dive under.

022

As they start to realize what you're doing, you have to already be going faster.

Power past as fast as you can.

023

As you go under, remember you still have to finish the job.

024

025

At this point, it's a drag race. The more speed you can build before this the easier finishing the pass will be.

026

Greg uses the angle of the berm like a starting hill to build more speed.

027

As you go by, start to carve back toward the outside slightly.

Head back in front of the rider you just passed.

028

At this point, you've committed to the final part of the pass.

029

030

Get in front and "shut the door" on the other guy.

031

Keep the speed going and get away as fast as you can, sights set on the next person to pass.

BLOCK PASS

The block pass is another fundamental pass you should have in your arsenal.

Carry as much speed as you can into the turn, going inside the rider ahead of you. You want to carve under and go past the other rider enough to be able to cut them off, but not so far that they can catch you with a high-low pass. Keep an eye on them under your arm if you can.

As you cut in front of the rider, go high enough to keep them from passing you, but not so high that you force them off the backside of the berm. These guys are your buddies, and you want them to stay that way. You have to see them every weekend and if you force them off the track don't think they won't return the favor.

As with any pass, these are descriptions of what to do when it's mainly you and another rider. Add more people and it becomes a little more complex, yet remains basically the same. You'll have to watch out for the others, perhaps pass them too, and keep an eye on anyone else who's ahead. Set your sights on them and get going!

Pedal into the turn later than the person you're passing if you can.

For the block pass, concentrate on getting into the turn fast enough to pass.

Go well inside the turn.

You won't have the starting hill effect of the berm, so you have to slip under and muscle your way past the other rider.

036

Start to carve up.

037

At this point, the person you're passing knows you are there and may try to cut you off.

038

You have to keep forcing your way up and past the other rider.

039

Keep pedaling.

040

Cut off the other rider.

041

Keep going toward the outside once you're in front.

042

When your back wheel is even with the other rider's front, you're almost home free.

Keep forcing your way toward the outside.

Shut the door as quickly as you can.

045

Pedal like crazy to keep your momentum going and increase your lead.

Here's where you can use the starting hill effect down the end of the berm.

046

Stay toward the outside, but not too far—you don't want the other rider to high-low pass you.

Set your sights on the next obstacle or rider and get there.

NUTRITION

Good nutrition goes a long way toward performing your best on the track. Eating a bunch of junk food is like running water in the gas tank of your car. It isn't fuel and won't get you very far. A lot of our normal diets consist of sugar and fat. It'd be easy to write a book on the subject, and there are a lot of them out there already. Read up if you want, but all it takes is a little common sense to make a big difference in your performance.

First of all, bag the candy bars and soda. Candy bars are pure sugar and calories, which just puts excess fat on your body. They're not a good source of fuel. Soda presents the same sugar problem, and adds carbonation, which can get in the way of your body's absorption of oxygen.

Drink plenty of water. Eight glasses of water are recommended for the average person, but some BMX pros drink well over twice that, more than a gallon of water a day. Water dissolves more bad stuff than any other substance on the planet. Your body is around 60 percent water, so make sure it has a plentiful supply to help keep it healthy.

I know a lot of tracks depend on concessions to make money, but take your own food to the track. If you want to support the track, show up for practice and volunteer to help maintain the track outside of practice and race days. Most track concession stands serve candy, hamburgers, and hot dogs, and some go the extra mile in serving chili cheese fries and nachos. All that stuff is bad for you and will give you nothing on race days. Take along a tuna sandwich from home and bring some carrots and apples to snack on.

Watch your carbohydrate intake. The body stores its preferred source of energy, glycogen, in the muscles. A certain amount of carbs will help maintain this. The average American diet, full of potatoes, pasta, and other carbohydrate-rich food has many times what even a serious athlete can use. Once your body has the carbohydrates it needs, it starts storing the excess as fat.

Stick with lean proteins, fruits, and vegetables. Turkey, chicken, lean beef, and even non-meat products like nuts and beans (tofu falls into the bean category) are all great sources of what your body needs to stay strong and rebuild. Watch fruit juices and fruit cups (the Jell-o type), as most of these are pure sugar, or close to it. Eat fresh fruit and vegetables whenever you can; salads are great at meals. These are all water-rich foods and will be high-quality fuel for your "tank."

You're now prepared to get out there and do your best racing. Now it's up to you to apply all this stuff and work on your skills and enjoy everything the sport of BMX has to offer.

INDEX

The World of BMX
ISBN 0-7603-1543-4

**Lines: The Snowboard
Photography of Sean Sullivan**
ISBN 0-7603-1678-3

**Freeestyle Motocross II:
Air Sickness**
ISBN 0-7603-1184-6

Mountain Bike Madness
ISBN 0-7603-1440-3

World of Whitewater Kayaking
ISBN 0-7603-1962-6

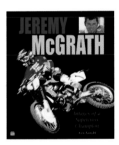

**Jeremy McGrath: Images of a
Supercross Champion**
ISBN 0-7603-2032-2

The Cars of Gran Turismo
ISBN 0-7603-1495-0

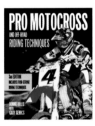

**Pro Motocross and Off-Road
Riding Techniques, 3rd Ed.**
ISBN 0-7603-1802-6

**The Cars of
The Fast and the Furious**
ISBN 0-7603-1551-5